IRISES

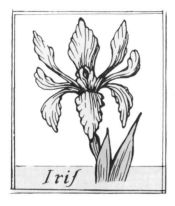

Iris

IRISES

SUSAN BERRY

A ROMANTIC HISTORY WITH A GUIDE TO CULTIVATION

RUNNING PRESS
Philadelphia, Pennsylvania

Copyright © 1992 by Inklink

Concept, design & editorial direction Simon Jennings.
Produced, edited, and designed at Inklink,
Greenwich, London, England.

Text by Susan Berry
Consultant Editor Brian Mathew
Designed by Simon Jennings
& Alan Marshall
Botanical illustrations by Julia Cobbold
Archive illustrations enhanced by
Robin Harris & David Day
Text edited by
Albert Jackson & Peter Leek

Published in The United States of America
by Running Press, Philadelphia, Pennsylvania

Text setting and computer make-up by Inklink, London.
Image generation by Blackheath Publishing Services, London.
Printed by Southsea International Press, Hong Kong.

Canadian representatives: General Publishing Co., Ltd.,
30 Lesmill Road, Don Mills, Ontario M3B 2T6.
International representatives: Worldwide Media Services, Inc.,
30 Montgomery Street, Jersey City, New Jersey 07302.

9 8 7 6 5 4 3 2 1
Digit on the right indicates the number of this printing.

Library of Congress Catalog Number 92-53691

ISBN 1-56138-141-1

This book may be ordered by mail from the publisher.
Please add $2.50 for postage and handling.
But try your bookstore first!
Running Press Book Publishers
125 South Twenty-Second Street
Philadelphia, Pennsylvania 19103

IRISES
A ROMANTIC HISTORY
WITH A GUIDE TO CULTIVATION
ARRANGED IN THREE CHAPTERS

CONTENTS

THE IRIS
Fair among the fairest
"Thou art the iris, fair among the fairest,
Who, armed with golden rod
And winged with celestial azure, bearest
The message of some God."
HENRY WADSWORTH LONGFELLOW (1807-82)

Introduction

For the broad expanses and widely different climates and soils of the American Continent, "There is no flower so universally adapted as the iris. It withstands equally the below-zero temperatures of Canadian winters and the hot scorching winds and prolonged droughts of the summers south of the Mason and Dixon *(sic)* line. From New Brunswick to Florida we find it the mainstay of the hardy garden…within the narrow confines of a town garden [any gardener] can have a range of color, a length of season and a wealth of beauty that cannot be surpassed by any other genus of plants." The author, John C. Wister, was, admittedly, biased, being the first president of the American Iris Society and one of the foremost breeders of irises. But his statement holds good today, as much as when he wrote his book, *The Iris*, in 1930.

Since then many more fascinating forms of iris have been bred, and the wealth of choice open to gardeners today is almost breathtaking. The genus *Iris* (part of the large *Iridaceae* family of flowering plants, which includes *Crocus, Gladiolus,* and *Freesia*) comprises some 200 species, let alone many thousands of varieties and hybrids. Not only is the choice of size, form, and color amazingly comprehensive, there are irises for almost every situation and climate, from mixed borders to alpine troughs and lakeside plantings. However, since irises vary considerably in their native habitats, care has to be taken to match the plant to the environment.

In this book, the main descriptions of the species, hybrids, and varieties are organized into various garden settings – border, waterside, and rock garden – to help the reader know what should be planted where.

DEDICATED TO
OUR ENVIRONMENT
WHICH SUFFERS
IN SILENCE

CHAPTER

I

IRISES IN HISTORY

I DREW MY BRIDE, BENEATH THE MOON,
ACROSS MY THRESHOLD; HAPPY HOUR!
BUT, AH, THE WALK THAT AFTERNOON
WE SAW THE WATER-FLAGS IN FLOWER!
FROM "THE SPIRIT'S EPOCHS" BY COVENTRY PATMORE 1823-1896

9

IRISES
by Hugo van der Goes (1435-82)
Detail from the painting,
THE ADORATION OF THE SHEPHERDS,
Uffizi, Florence.

SOURCES OF IRISES

THE IRIS IS NAMED AFTER THE GREEK GODDESS of the Rainbow or Messenger of the Gods, who was depicted as "A radiant maiden borne in swift flight on golden wings. Among her duties was that of leading the souls of dead women to the Elysian fields, and as a token of that faith the Greeks planted purple iris on the graves of women," according to Hollingsworth in his *Flower Chronicles*.

The iris flower has a long and colorful history, and has been appreciated by many people in many different lands. In the Yemen mountains, Muslim soldiers carried irises with them to plant on the graves of their fallen comrades, and even today irises are found growing wild in fields where great battles, long since forgotten, were once fought.

The iris was well known in Britain by the sixteenth century. John Gerard in his famous *Herbal* wrote: "There be many kinds of iris or flouer de Luce, whereof some are tall and great and some little, small and low. Some smell exceeding sweet in the roote, some have not anie smell at al; some flowers are without any smell and some with; some have one colour, some have many colours mixed." Gerard himself grew at least 16 different forms of iris in his own garden, several of which were clearly from other countries as he listed them as "the great flouer de luce of Dalmatia...the wilde Turkie flouer de luce, the little French flouer de luce...and the variable flouer de luce of Constantinople."

More than 400 years ago, the iris was sufficiently popular for the great Renaissance botanist Carolus Clusius to be able to list nine different species from southern Europe, including *Iris alata, I. sisyrinchium*, and *I. lusitanica*.

IRIS ASIATICA CAERULEA
(or latifolia major) from the
RARORIUM PLANTARUM HISTORIA 1601,
by Carolus Clusius (1524-1609)

11

ORIGINS OF IRISES

IRISES ARE NATIVE TO A WIDE RANGE OF COUNTRIES in the northern hemisphere, and different species flourish in remarkably diverse conditions, from the freezing expanses of Alaska to the scorchingly hot deserts of central Asia. Broadly speaking, their origins can be classified as North American, Asian, and European.

IRIS VERSICOLOR (BLUE FLAG)
FROM PLANTAE ET PAPILIONES RARIORES, 1748-59, by
George Dionysius Ehret (1708-70).

North American irises

On the Atlantic side you will find *Iris versicolor, I. virginica,* and *I. cristata* – one of the few crested irises to grow naturally in the U.S.A. *Iris prismatica,* a unique species of iris, also hails from the Eastern States. Farther south, *Iris fulva* and *I. brevicaulis* (syn. *I. foliosa*) flourish, and the Pacific coast is home to *I. douglasiana,* one of the species in the Californicae group of irises.

IRIS VIRGINICA

European irises

All along the Mediterranean you can find a wide range of irises. From Austria and Eastern Europe comes the little purple-flowered *Iris pumila,* one of the parents of the short-stemmed bearded iris. In Hungary, *I. variegata* grows wild; and in the Balkans and Italy, *I. pallida,* with its lavender-blue flowers, is a native. In low, wet land, almost everywhere in Europe, you can find *I. pseuda-corus,* the native British flag, with its tall sheaves of sword-shaped leaves and yellow flowers.

IRIS VARIEGATA

Asian irises

Among the irises from the Asian continent are some of the beard-less irises, including *Iris orientalis, I. laevigata* (from Japan & Siberia), *I. japonica* from China, and *Iris tectorum* from Japan and China. Western and Central Asia are the home of the Regelia irises, and also of the bulbous group of iris-es called Junos. "Of these, *Iris bucharica,* from nearby Bokhara, is best known in American gar-dens. It is easily distinguished by the yellow-and-white flowers appearing in the axils of the foliage like miniature corn." (Mitchell, *Iris for Every Garden*)

IRIS JAPONICA

13

THE IRIS IN ART

THE OLDEST KNOWN IMAGE OF THE IRIS appears in a fresco of the Priest King at the Palace of Minos at Knossos, but the iris has been much appreciated by many different civilizations throughout the centuries. Early medieval lettering in illuminated manuscripts frequently features iris-like shapes in the letter designs, and irises in various forms have cropped up in paintings since the Renaissance, when it was frequently used as a symbol to depict the birth of Christ.

One of the earliest paintings of irises was by the Dutch artist, Hugo van der Goes, in 1475. Albrecht Dürer's picture of the *Madonna in the Garden,* painted in 1508, features irises very prominently, and Dürer also made an exquisite watercolor study of an iris specifically for that painting. The Dutch and Flemish flower and still-life painters of the sixteenth and seventeenth centuries, such as Johannes and Ambrosius Bosschaert and Osias Beert, frequently included irises in their groups of plants, and they have been popular subjects in paintings ever since.

In the nineteenth century, Cezanne, Renoir, and van Gogh all found inspiration in the delicate flowers and architectural shapes of irises, either for still-life compositions or as subjects growing naturally in the garden. One famous example is van Gogh's painting of irises in a border at the asylum in Saint Remy.

Stylized depictions of irises have also been widely used in ceramics by many different cultures, notably the Persians and the Chinese. The Japanese clearly admired its form as much as its color, and the curving shapes of the petals have been an inspiration to textile artists over the centuries, particularly to William Morris, the doyen of the Arts and Crafts movement, who used them many times in his stylized fabric patterns.

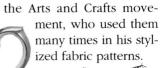

14

Vase with violet irises (1889)
Vincent van Gogh (1853-90)
VINCENT VAN GOGH MUSEUM, AMSTERDAM
*Van Gogh was inspired by the iris
borders at the asylum at Saint-
Rémy where he made several
paintings, including this still life.*

Iris design, detail *(c.1887)*
William Morris & Co. Workshop
VICTORIA & ALBERT MUSEUM, LONDON
*One of the most successful and
popular designs of J. H. Dearle
(1860-1932), Morris's pupil and
colleague. This design is often
mistakenly attributed to William
Morris himself.*

15

Iris spuria and I. sibirica
by Emanuel Sweerts (1552-1612)
FROM THE 1612 FLORILEGIUM
*The Florilegium was compiled by
Sweerts, and was first printed in
Frankfurt am Main in 1612. It is one
of the most sumptuous early books of
flora, and contains engravings of
many iris species.*

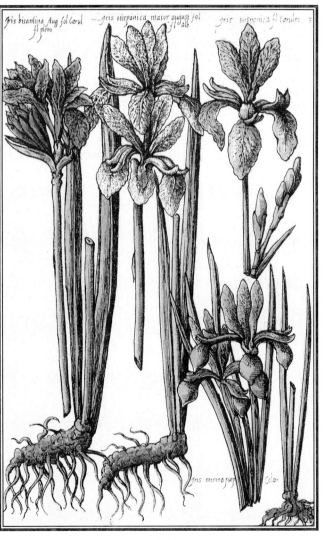

THE IRIS IN HERALDRY

THE HERALDIC FLEUR-DE-LIS almost certainly derives from the iris flower. According to John Guillim, in *A Display of Heraldrie*, published in 1610, the fleur-de-lis "is in Latine called Iris." Its origins derive apparently from the time of Clovis I, King of the Franks in the sixth century AD, whose army was being pursued by the Goths and was trapped by a bend in the river at Cologne. Clovis caught sight of yellow irises growing far out in the water, and realized that the river had to be shallow enough at that point for his army to cross to safety. Having escaped, he showed his debt to the iris by adopting the flower as his emblem. In the twelfth century, the emblem was revived by the French king, Louis VII, who adopted it as his own during the Crusades, whereupon it was christened the "Fleur de Louis," or fleur-de-lis.

According to Hollingsworth in his *Flower Chronicles,* so potent a symbol of the monarchy had the fleur-de-lis become in France by the eighteenth century that the Revolutionaries, in 1789, set out to obliterate it, chipping it off buildings and tearing it down from draperies. Men were guillotined for no more than wearing a fleur-de-lis on their clothes or jewellery. The iris has also been called the flower of chivalry: "a sword for its leaf, and a lily for its heart," and the three points of the fleur-de-lis are reputed to stand for faith, wisdom, and valor.

17

THE USEFUL IRIS

FROM THE EARLIEST TIMES, the iris has had a number of medicinal and other uses. The Greeks and Romans used the dried rhizomes in perfumery as well as in medicine, and in Macedonia and Corinth irises were employed to flavor various ointments. The seeds have been used as a substitute for coffee, and the leaves for thatch and as seating material for chairs.

Iris roots

The most widely used product of the iris, however, is orris root, taken from the rhizomes of *I. pallida* and *I. florentina*, which was considered to provide a cure for scrofula as well as certain blood and lung disorders.

The rhizomes of *Iris florentina, I. pallida,* and *I. germanica* are dug up in summer and trimmed, peeled, and sun-dried, strung up like beads and hung out on lines like washing. After the roots have dried, they are stored for up to two years, developing a delightfully strong odor of fresh violets.

The roots of *Iris florentina* (described by William Turner in the sixteenth century as "full of joints, hard and well-smelling, whyche are cut in little shives or cakes, and are dried in the shadow and are put on a threde and so kept") were also used as a remedy for "a pimpled or saucie face" and for putting among linen, for making beads for rosaries, as teething rings for infants, and for chewing to whiten the teeth.

Dioscorides, in his *De Materia Medica* in the first century AD, discussed the use of iris root as a remedy for removing freckles. He also recommended it for a condition termed "mickle hreak" (phlegm in the throat to us):

18

"Let him take the root of this wort [*Iris germanica*], pounded small, by weight ten pennies, give to drink to the sufferer, fasting, in lithe beer, four draughts for three days, till that be healed." A physician to the Duke of Somerset in the seventeenth century suggested making a broth of iris, "sodden with wyne," as a mouthwash. Used as a poultice, orris root was reputed to be good for tumors and ulcers, and even for healing broken bones.

Rooftop irises

Although a range of perfumes and drugs has been made from different species of iris, and various parts of the plant, one of the most fascinating stories comes from Japan. Many centuries ago, at the time of a great famine, people were ordered to stop growing ornamental plants in their gardens and to cultivate only those which were edible. The Japanese women, who made their face powder from a certain kind of iris, decided that they could not do without it, and to get around the edict they grew the irises on the thatched roofs of their houses. To the present day, this iris, now known as *I. tectorum*, can be seen growing on the roofs of houses in Japan. Curiously enough, *Iris florentina* is also grown on roofs in Normandy, in France, where early dwarf bearded irises are also grown on tops of walls.

Iris florentina
The plant from which the orris root is derived, is seen here in bloom.

19

THE IRIS BREEDERS

Much APPRECIATED FOR THE EXQUISITE BEAUTY of their form and color, irises have been an inspiration for many different cultures and civilizations at different periods. The Greeks and Hebrews were the first recorded iris worshippers, more than 2000 years ago, and since then many plant collectors and breeders have fallen under the iris's spell. One of the earliest known iris fanciers was Carolus Clusius, some 400 years ago, who was able to describe no fewer than 28 different tall bearded irises and commented that "long experience has taught me that iris grown from seed vary in a wonderful way."

Of all the forms of iris, the tall bearded ones, a cross between the wild iris of Italy, *Iris pallida,* and the wild iris of Hungary, *I. variegata*, have most excited the

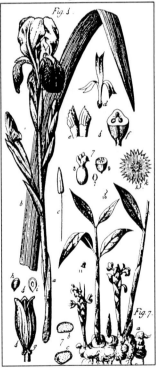

interest of plant breeders over the years. Many hybrids of the two species were found in nature, and assiduously collected by European nurserymen more than 200 years ago. By the turn of the century, seeds were being transported to the United States, where an American nurseryman in Long Island first cataloged some 20 distinct forms. The enthusiasm for these lovely irises spread rapidly, but in both Britain and the States scientific breeding did not get under way until Sir Michael Foster, Professor of Physiology at Cambridge University in England, introduced some newly discovered irises from the East into a planned breeding program.

An engraving from the
ICONOGRAPHIC ENCYCLOPEDIA OF
SCIENCE, LITERATURE, AND ART,
originally published in 1851.

An enthusiastic collector in the 1880s and 1890s, Foster brought back from trips to Asia the first tall bearded irises with branching stems and large flowers, *Iris cypriana*. Crossing this with *I. pallida*, he created hybrids with tremendous potential, in terms of flower color and size, as well as branching qualities. His garden at Shelford, near Cambridge, amply demonstrated the virtues of irises – he collected and grew all the species he could, and introduced a number of new ones. He also inspired W.R. Dykes, a master at Charterhouse School, to follow him in his passion. Dykes grew numerous iris species in his garden at Godalming, Surrey, and rapidly became a world authority. In 1913, he published the standard work on irises, *The Genus Iris*.

At about the same time, a French company, Vilmorin-Andrieux et Cie, were also experimenting with plants brought back from Asia. They had brought seedlings belonging to the collector Verdier after his death in 1900, and started the revival of interest in irises in France, producing celebrated cultivars such as 'Ambassadeur', 'Ballerina', 'Magnifica', and 'Medrano'.

In America, the popularity of the iris was greatly enhanced by the work of Bertrand H. Farr, who imported immense collections of irises from Europe around the turn of the century. He put his first iris seedlings on the market in 1908, winning the highest prize at the San Francisco Exposition in 1915. His efforts prompted Miss Grace Sturtevant of Massachusetts to emulate him, and among the first varieties she put into commerce were 'Afterglow', 'Queen Caterina', and 'Shekinah'. In 1920, the American Iris Society came into being, and the number of iris breeders proliferated, Mr. William Mohr of California being one of the most prominent. The national societies in England, France, and the U.S.A. have since done a great deal to promote interest in breeding good strains of iris and have helped to keep members in close touch with what others are producing.

IRIS ENTHUSIASTS

GERTRUDE JEKYLL

GARDENERS from Europe, the U.S.A., and Japan have included among their ranks some notable iris enthusiasts, including the great gardening writers Vita Sackville-West and Gertrude Jekyll (see page 24). As a plant for the gardens at her home, Sissinghurst Castle, Vita regarded the iris as second only in importance to the rose. She grew tall bearded irises in the rose gardens, where they made the perfect companion plant, providing color and foliage interest at times when the roses were not blooming. Gertrude Jekyll was equally fond of them, and liked to plant them with lupins in the mixed border.

A colorful mixed iris border at the height of perfection
Although there is an iris in bloom for every month of the year, midsummer is the time when most of them are at their peak.

22

CHAPTER

II

I RISES FOR YOUR GARDEN

AND FLOWERS AZURE, BLACK, AND STREAKED WITH GOLD,
FAIRER THAN ANY WAKENED EYES BEHOLD.
AND NEARER TO THE RIVER'S TREMBLING EDGE.
THERE GREW BROAD FLAG-FLOWERS, PURPLE, PRANKED WITH WHITE

FROM "THE REVOLT OF ISLAM," 1818
PERCY BYSSHE SHELLEY 1792-1882

IRISES FOR ALL SEASONS

IN EDWARDIAN TIMES, IRISES WERE A FEATURE in the gardens of many stately homes and were highly enough regarded for special beds to be devoted to the different species, hybrids, and varieties. Gertrude Jekyll (see page 22), famous for her exquisite flower borders, gives the plans for a typical iris and lupin bed in her book *Colour Schemes for the Flower Garden* (1908). A similar iris border, suitably scaled down, could easily be created in a small town garden, by carefully selecting forms that flower at different times of the year. In fact, it is perfectly possible to create an iris border for all seasons. The chart opposite gives a choice of species and colors with their appropriate flowering times.

Although many of the species iris have only a short flowering season, most of the hybrids have a much longer blooming time – most of them flower for three to four weeks. Recent innovations in breeding have created repeat-flowering (remontant) strains that will flower twice a year if given a little encouragement in the form of adequate feeding and watering.

Tall bearded irises at the Royal Botanic Gardens, Kew.

IRISES THROUGHOUT THE YEAR

Type	Flowering season	Color	Height
Bulbous Irises			
Iris bakerana	Early spring	Blue	4in
Iris danfordiae	Early spring	Yellow	4in
Iris histrioides	Mid spring	Blue	4in
Iris reticulata	Mid spring	Purple	4in
Juno Irises			
Iris bucharica	Late spring	White/yellow	15in
Iris graeberiana	Late spring	Light blue	12in
Bearded Irises			
Iris chamaeiris	Late spring	Yellow/purple	6-8in
Iris pumila	Late spring	Various	4in
Iris pallida	Early summer	Pale blue	4in
Iris variegata	Early summer	Yellow/brown	18in
Aril Irises			
Iris hoogiana	Early summer	Blue	18-30in
Iris susiana	Early summer	Grey/purple	18in
Crested Irises			
Iris cristata	Early to mid summer	Lilac-blue	3-4in
Iris tectorum	Early to mid summer	Blue/white	10in
Beardless Irises			
Iris versicolor	Early summer	Blue	18in
Iris virginica	Early summer	Blue	18-24in
Iris chrysographes	Mid summer	Purple	15in
Iris foetidissima	Mid summer	Purple	18in
Iris brevicaulis	Mid summer	Purple	12in
Iris kaempferi	Mid summer	Purple	24-30in
Iris laevigata	Mid summer	Blue/white	24-30in
Iris pseudacorus	Mid summer	Yellow	30-60in
Iris sibirica	Mid summer	Blue	28in
Iris forrestii	Mid summer	Yellow	18in
Iris fulva	Mid summer	Rust	24-30in
Iris dichotoma	Late summer	Lilac/white	24in
Iris unguicularis	Autumn to spring	Lilac	4in

"Singular and beautiful colour"
"Irises have been compared to Orchids, and those who delight in singular and beautiful colour, and to whom greenhouses and hot-houses are denied, may find a substitute for Orchids in Irises."
BY WILLIAM ROBINSON, FROM "THE ENGLISH FLOWER GARDEN," 1892

WHAT IS AN IRIS?

IRISES ARE DIVIDED INTO SEVERAL DIFFERENT GROUPS, but there are two principal types: bearded irises and beardless ones. Although all the bearded irises are more or less similar, the beardless group embraces a variety of types.

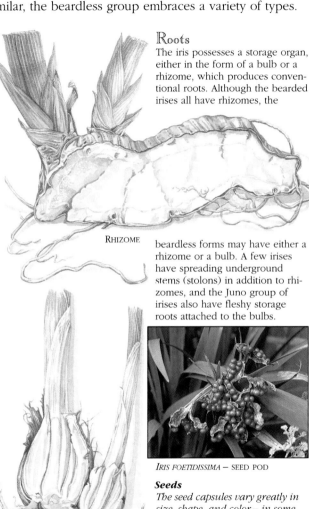

Roots

The iris possesses a storage organ, either in the form of a bulb or a rhizome, which produces conventional roots. Although the bearded irises all have rhizomes, the beardless forms may have either a rhizome or a bulb. A few irises have spreading underground stems (stolons) in addition to rhizomes, and the Juno group of irises also have fleshy storage roots attached to the bulbs.

RHIZOME

IRIS FOETIDISSIMA – SEED POD

Seeds

The seed capsules vary greatly in size, shape, and color – in some forms of iris they are an attractive feature in their own right. Iris foetidissima, for example, has huge seed pods in late autumn, which split open to reveal scores of orange seeds.

BULB

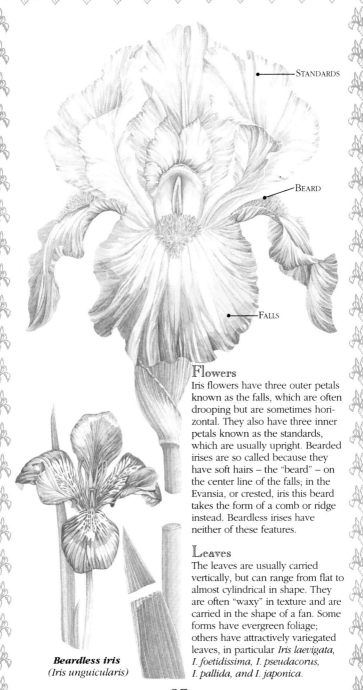

STANDARDS

BEARD

FALLS

Beardless iris
(Iris unguicularis)

Flowers

Iris flowers have three outer petals known as the falls, which are often drooping but are sometimes horizontal. They also have three inner petals known as the standards, which are usually upright. Bearded irises are so called because they have soft hairs – the "beard" – on the center line of the falls; in the Evansia, or crested, iris this beard takes the form of a comb or ridge instead. Beardless irises have neither of these features.

Leaves

The leaves are usually carried vertically, but can range from flat to almost cylindrical in shape. They are often "waxy" in texture and are carried in the shape of a fan. Some forms have evergreen foliage; others have attractively variegated leaves, in particular *Iris laevigata, I. foetidissima, I. pseudacorus, I. pallida,* and *I. japonica.*

27

IRISES FOR BORDERS

IRISES ARE AN INVALUABLE ELEMENT IN ANY MIXED BORDER and the smaller bearded irises make excellent front-of-the-border plants. Their handsome sword-shaped leaves provide an architectural contrast when planted with spring bulbs and summer-flowering perennials. Irises of all forms can be used to provide a continuity of flower color throughout the seasons.

Iris variegata
A species bearded iris (see page 31) from which many of the bearded hybrids have been produced.

Bearded irises

Bearded irises fall into two main categories, known respectively as the Pogoniris group and the Aril species and hybrids. Both groups need good well-drained soil, and sun to flourish, but the Aril forms are not generally hardy.

Bearded (Pogoniris) irises are sub-categorized into the following groups: miniature dwarf bearded (MDB), median irises, comprising standard dwarf bearded (SDB), intermediate bearded (IB), and tall bearded irises (TB).

The miniature and standard dwarf bearded irises are most suitable for the rock garden and are dealt with on page 51. They can also be used to edge a border.

IRIS 'SUDELEY'

Intermediate bearded irises

These flower in late-spring/early summer. About 16-40in (40-90cm) tall, they have two or more branches to the stems and at least six flowers. They were bred from tall bearded irises crossed with the small species, *Iris pumila*. Two other groups of iris, the miniature tall bearded and the border bearded, flower slightly later – in early to mid summer. They are much the same height as the IB forms, but carry eight flowers rather than six. The border bearded irises are similar, but have larger flowers and somewhat thicker stems.

Among the IB cultivars worth trying are: 'Annikins,' deep bluish-purple; 'Sudeley,' blue and purple; 'Sarah Taylor,' cream and yellow; 'Bold Print', purple-edged white standards and falls; 'Brown Lassoo', butterscotch standards and brown-edged violet falls; 'Chiltern Gold', bright yellow; 'Langport Wren', deep reddish-black; 'Razzmataz', lilac and white, with brown markings on the falls.

IRIS 'SARAH TAYLOR'

IRIS 'RAZZMATAZ'

29

IRIS 'BRIGHT FORECAST'

IRIS 'FOTHERGILL'

IRIS 'GALILEE'

Tall bearded irises

These were developed principally from crossing *Iris pallida* with *I. variegata*. Most TB irises have seven flowers to a stem – and recently remontant forms have been bred successfully, which give better value since the normal flowering period is fairly short.

Among the many colors in the range are: 'Black Swan', with reddish-black flowers and a brown beard; 'Bright Forecast', with yellow standards and falls; 'Caramba', with lemon standards and white falls with purple markings; 'Cliffs of Dover', creamy-white standards and falls; 'Fothergill', peachy apricot with an orange beard; 'Galilee', which is pale blue with dark veining and a yellow beard; 'Paradise Falls', with dark reddish-purple standards and paler falls; 'Peach Frost', with apricot standards and white-and-apricot falls, 'Shepherd's Delight', with pink standards and falls; and 'Vanity', which has light-pink standards and a coral-colored beard.

IRIS PALLIDA

Species bearded irises

The iris from which many of the bearded hybrids have been produced is *Iris pallida*, with lavender-blue flowers and a yellow beard. A variegated form, *I. p.* 'Aurea Variegata', has attractively striped yellow-and-green leaves.

Iris variegata has from three to six flowers per stem, with yellow standards and falls that are heavily marked in brown, with almost tigerlike striping (see page 28).

Iris germanica, the common German flag (which actually originates in the Mediterranean region), has violet-blue flowers in early summer. *I. g.* 'Florentina' is a white-flowered variety with scented, slightly bluish-white flowers.

IRIS GERMANICA

IRIS GERMANICA 'FLORENTINA'

IRIS PALLIDA 'AUREA VARIEGATA'

31

IRIS KOROLKOWII

IRIS HOOGIANA

IRIS STOLONIFERA

Regelia & Oncocyclus irises

These two groups of iris are rhizomatous and have beard-ed flowers. They tend to be difficult to cultivate successful-ly and are mostly grown in frames, especially in areas that suffer from wet summers. They need well-drained, fairly rich soil and a dry period after flowering. Regelia irises differ from Oncocyclus in having bearded standards and falls, and having two flowers, rather than one, per stem. Hybrids between the groups are known as Regeliocyclus irises.

Regelia irises

Iris korolkowii flowers in late spring or early summer, with creamy-white or light-purple flowers with dark veining. The plant stems are about 16-24in (40-60cm) tall; *I. korolkowii* is not hardy.

Iris hoogiana has two or three large, scented, delicately veined, lilac flowers with a yellow beard, growing on each 16-24in (40-60cm) stem in early summer.

Iris stolonifera has flowering stems between 12 and 24in (30-60cm) tall, and two or three large flowers in midsum-mer. The flowers are brown-and-purple, with a yellowish beard. There are hybrids avail-able between this species and *I. hoogiana*.

Oncocyclus irises

These irises originally hailed from Iran and adjacent countries. According to W.R. Dykes, "they are no less weird and wonderful than the name, Oncocyclus, of which no explanation has ever been given." They are important as parents of some particularly attractive hybrids.

The following species are particularly well known:

Iris iberia has large, solitary flowers, usually with white standards and heavily brown-veined falls. It is quite small, growing to about 6-8in (15-20cm) tall, and flowers in late spring.

Iris haynei has large dusky-lilac flowers that are veined and spotted in dark brown, with darker standards. It flowers in mid spring and grows to about 8-10in (20-30cm) tall.

Iris samariae grows to about 10-12in (25-30cm) tall, with large creamy-white purple-veined falls and pinkish-purple standards. It flowers in mid spring.

Iris susiana is also called the Mourning Iris, and is the best known of the Oncocyclus irises. It is unknown in the wild and was probably cultivated by the Ottoman Turks in their gardens more than 400 years ago. The flowers are marked with heavy brownish-purple veins, with a deep brownish-black beard, blooming in late spring on 12-16in (30-40cm) stems.

IRIS HAYNEI

IRIS SAMARIAE

IRIS SUSIANA

33

IRIS BUCHARICA

IRIS MAGNIFICA

IRIS 'WARLSIND'

Juno irises

This group of bulbous irises is found in western and central Asia, and on the shores of the Mediterranean. The bulbs have fleshy feeding roots; and the flowers have tiny down-turned standards, and prominent crests and falls. The leaves are deeply channeled, and the flowers develop from the bases of the leaves that grow up the stem.

Juno irises need sun and good drainage, with some moisture during the growing season and a good baking in summer. If the fleshy feeding roots are damaged, the plants may fail to flower, so care should be taken not to disturb them.

These particular irises are not as commonly grown in the United States as some of the other groups, but two species in particular, *Iris persica* and *I. alata,* with vanilla-scented flowers, are hardy in New England, for example. According to Mitchell in *Iris for Every Garden,* "A correspondent near Buffalo writes that if you give the Junos a good stiff soil and leave them alone, they will perform quite nicely."

Of the well-known species, *Iris bucharica* has branching stems about 12in (30cm) tall with white yellow-bladed flowers in the axils of the leaves in spring. A form with deep-gold flowers is known as *I. orchioides.*

Iris magnifica, which grows to about 12-24in (30-60cm) tall, is easily cultivated. It has up to seven white or pale-violet flowers with a central yellow patch on each fall in late spring. The leaves are mid-green, glossy, and channeled. Two hardy hybrids are *I.* 'Sindpers', which is slightly smaller and has greenish-blue flowers, and *I.* 'Warlsind', with yellow-and-blue flowers on a 10-14in (25-35cm) stem.

Spuria irises

This particular group of irises is found in Europe and western Asia, Asia Minor, and Kashmir. The name "spuria" apparently means "bastard", which seems to be the wrong description for the true species and hybrids of impeccable parentage that make up this group.

Spurias need full sun and a lot of moisture during the growing season, but benefit from dry summers. Planting should be carried out in early autumn, with the rhizomes laid just below the soil surface. Although these irises do particularly well along the Pacific Coast, they will grow as far north as Portland, Maine.

In the garden, they look best planted in large groups. Being tall, they should be positioned near the back of a herbaceous border. They also have the advantage of attractive foliage.

Iris orientalis (syn. *I. ochroleuca*), a native of Asia Minor, grows very tall – up to 5ft (1.2m) – with white, or almost white, flowers. *Iris monnieri* is very similar, but has yellow flowers. Both flower in summer.

The species from which the group takes its name, *I. spuria,* is very variable, with two to five-flowers in either pale blue, mid-blue, bluish-purple, yellow, or white, held on 3ft (90cm) branching stems. It prefers moist soil and blooms in midsummer.

Iris crocea (syn. *I. aurea*) is reputed to be a native of Kashmir. The flowers are very large and deep golden yellow in color, with erect, slightly crinkled standards. *I. crocea* grows to about 5ft (1.5m) and tends to flower in midsummer. It makes a good subject for a sunny border.

IRIS SPURIA

IRIS ORIENTALIS (SYN. I. OCHROLEUCA)

IRIS MONNIERI

35

IRIS 'PURPLE SENSATION'

IRIS 'WEDGWOOD'

IRISES FOR BORDERS

Dutch, English, & Spanish irises

These are all bulbous irises. Bulbs should be planted about 2in (5cm) deep and about 7in (18cm) apart.

Dutch irises

These are hybrids of *I. tingitana*, which grows to about 24in (60cm) tall, and *I. xiphium*. For flowering in early to mid summer, the bulbs must be planted in early autumn.

Among the popular cultivars today are: 'Blue Elegance', with purple standards and blue falls; and 'Bronze Queen', which has yellowish bronze flowers, as the name suggests; 'Purple Sensation', which is deep purple with yellow markings; 'Symphony', with white-and-yellow flowers on 24in (60cm) tall stems; 'Wedgwood', with blue-and-white flowers, with a yellow flash; 'White Excelsior', which has white flowers from spring to early summer, with a yellow stripe down each fall; and 'Professor Blaw', which is a particularly good dark-blue form.

IRIS 'WHITE EXCELSIOR'

36

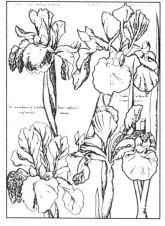

English iris
*Studies of garden varieties of
Iris xiphioides (now I. latifolia)
from the FLORILEGIUM of 1612, by
Emanuel Sweerts (1552-1612).*

English irises

Iris latifolia (formerly known as
I. xiphioides), commonly called
the English iris, was wrongly
thought to be a native of England.
In fact, it grows wild in the
Pyrenees. Whatever its origins, it
does well along the northwest
Pacific Coast and in coastal British
Columbia.

Iris latifolia needs a well-
drained sunny position where
frost will not damage the leaves,
and much richer soil than the
other irises in this group. The
species is quite tall – about 30in
(80cm) – and bears one or two
deep blue-violet flowers with a
central yellow stripe on each fall.
Among the currently grown varieties are 'Blue Giant', with darker
flecked bluish-purple standards
and dark-blue falls, and 'Mont
Blanc', with pure-white flowers.

Spanish irises

These need a sunny, well-drained
position that is sufficiently sheltered to avoid frost damage to the
young leaves, which appear
before the flowers some time in
early spring. Nurseries often
describe these irises simply as
Spanish irises, without giving any
named cultivars.

The principal species is *Iris
xiphium*, which has one or two
blue-violet flowers in mid to late
spring on stems up to 24in (60cm)
tall. Good named forms include:
'Praecox', which flowers slightly
earlier, with large blue flowers;
'Lusitanica', with yellow flowers;
and 'Battandieri', with white-and-
yellow flowers.

IRIS LATIFOLIA

IRIS XIPHIUM

37

IRIS JAPONICA

IRIS MILESII

IRIS TECTORUM

IRISES FOR BORDERS

Evansia or crested irises

The main feature of this group of irises is the frilly crest on the falls. They prefer slightly moister conditions than bearded irises, and are generally easy to grow. However, some species are tender, and need greenhouse treatment in colder climates. These irises were named after Thomas Evans, who introduced *Iris japonica*, one of the species, to cultivation in Britain.

Iris confusa is a native of China. This iris is a vigorous clump-forming plant with fans of broad leaves. It has a widely branching flower stem which, during late spring, bears a succession of lilac or yellow-spotted white flowers with a yellow crest.

Iris japonica, which, as the name suggests, comes from Japan, has fans of similar glossy leaves, and produces its pale-lilac or white ruffled flowers, adorned with a violet-edged orange crest on each fall, in late spring. It, too, needs a sunny, sheltered position and has a longer flowering season than most irises.

Iris milesii has branched flowering stems about 12-30in (30-75cm) tall with lavender flowers that have deeper-purple, mottled falls and a yellow crest. The flowers appear in succession over several weeks. It does well in an open sunny border and sets seed freely.

Iris tectorum, the Japanese roof iris, has fans of broad sword-shaped leaves. It bears clusters of two to three lilac flowers, with darker veins and blotches and a white crest. It needs a sunny, sheltered position, but is frost-hardy. It grows to about l2in (30cm) tall. There is also a pure-white form, 'Alba'.

Bog & waterside irises

THERE ARE SEVERAL VERY BEAUTIFUL SPECIES OF IRIS that prefer moist soil, and some that even prefer to have their roots immersed in water. Among the best known of these are some of the Siberian irises, the Japanese irises, and the common British flag, *Iris pseudacorus*. It is well worth creating a small pool or bog garden simply for the opportunity of growing these irises, which are among the most attractive to be found anywhere.

Iris virginica
This is a versatile species that grows equally well in boggy soil or with its feet in water.

39

IRIS ENSATA (I. KAEMPFERI)

IRIS ENSATA (I. KAEMPFERI) JAPANESE HYBRID

BOG IRISES

A permanently damp area of ground in a garden will support a variety of plants and attract wild-life. The appropriate choice of iris will provide natural-looking foliage and attractive color during the flowering seasoning.

Collected and hybridized for centuries in Japan, *Iris kaempferi* (now correctly called *I. ensata*) needs moist, lime-free soil to thrive. It makes the ideal subject for planting close to a pond or pool, and will also do well in about 2in (5cm) of water. It prefers full sun, but will cope perfectly well with partial shade.

Iris kaempferi carries three or four dark-purple flowers with narrow standards and wide falls on a stem 3ft (90cm) tall, appearing in mid to late summer. There are cultivars to be had in a range of colors – white, violet, pink, blue, and red – and sometimes in combinations of these colors. There is a particularly elegant white form called 'Alba', and one with attractively striped leaves called 'Variegata'. 'Sorcerer's Triumph' is a double white form with reddish purple veining, and there is also a very dark purple form called 'The Great Mogul'.

Two other species that grow well in boggy soil are *Iris versicolor* and *I. virginica* (which will also do well with its feet in water). They are similar in appearance to each other, and both are native to the States. Although both species have blue or violet flowers, those of *I. virginica* have a more conspicuous bright-yellow blotch on the falls. *Iris versicolor* 'Kermesina' is a rich wine-red color, and there are also pink shades known as 'Rosea'. A good white form is *I. virginica* 'Alba', and there are also white forms of *I. versicolor*.

IRIS VERSICOLOR

Louisiana irises

The native irises of the swamps of the southern United States, the Louisiana group of irises, flower in spring or summer. They do well in a bog garden, provided they have generous applications of well-rotted manure in the growing season. But they will also thrive in a mixed herbaceous border if provided with a rich, moist neutral or acid soil. Louisiana irises have a great following, and there are many hybrids and varieties in a wide range of colors.

Iris brevicaulis *(syn I. foliosa) has several flowerheads of large violet-blue flowers, with smaller standards and larger falls in spring. They appear in the axils of the leaves and at the top of the flowering stem.*

41

Siberian irises

There are two species and many hybrids in this group of irises. They grow well in any good garden soil, but look particularly attractive in large groups at the edge of a pool or lake. However, they prefer not to be waterlogged and need rich soil. The leaves are an additional attraction, being slender, long, and arching.

The main species, *I. sibirica*, has branching stems 3ft (90cm) tall, that bear six or eight purplish-blue flowers during midsummer. The falls are splashed with white and gold.

There are many hybrids between *I. sibirica* and the related *I. sanguinea*, and a number of named cultivars. A new form, called 'White Swirl', was introduced in the 1950s. It has more open, flatter flowers, as does 'Heavenly Blue', which is light-blue in color.

New cultivars developed in the last couple of decades have even-better flowers and foliage.

Remontant Siberian irises are now being bred that flower in late spring to early summer and again in autumn.

IRIS SIBIRICA

IRIS SIBIRICA 'WHITE SWIRL'

IRIS SIBIRICA 'HEAVENLY BLUE'

WATERSIDE IRISES

There are many varieties which do well with their feet in water and some types are equally at home either in boggy margins or with their roots totally submerged.

The true water-loving iris is *I. laevigata*, which does best with its feet in about 2in (5cm) of water, and its roots deep in rich soil. It has two to four violet-blue flowers on an 18in (45cm) stem. There are several varieties, including 'Variegata', with powder-blue flowers and handsomely striped leaves; 'Alba', which has pure-white flowers; and 'Atropurpurea', with deep reddish-purple flowers.

IRIS LAEVIGATA

Some double-flowered forms of *Iris laevigata* exist with standards that are as large as the falls. These include 'Midnight', with navy-blue flowers with a white line on each petal; and 'Snowdrift', which is pure white in color.

Iris pseudacorus, the native British flag, is taller than the other water-loving irises – about 30-60in (75-150cm) – and has up to 12 bright-yellow flowers in midsummer. There is a white form, 'Alba', which is less vigorous; and another, with larger golden-yellow flowers, called 'Golden Queen'.

IRIS PSEUDACORUS

Iris pseudacorus and *I. ensata* have been hybridized to produce attractive golden-flowered versions with brown veining. Two such varieties are 'Chance Beauty' and 'Aich-nokagayaki'. 'Holden Clough' is also a hybrid of *I. pseudacorus*

Iris versicolor will grow in about 2in (5cm) of water.

Iris prismatica, a native of the Atlantic coast of North America, is normally found in swampy ground or damp fields. It has slender grassy leaves and smallish light-violet flowers, on stems up to 30in (75cm) tall, in midsummer. There is also a white form, 'Alba'.

IRIS 'HOLDEN CLOUGH'

Chrysographes irises

These are very similar to the Siberian irises, but are less lime-tolerant, and they, too, flower in summer.

Iris chrysographes has narrow grass-like leaves and 14in (35cm) stems that bear blue or dark-purple flowers with gold markings on the falls. The variety called 'Rubella' has very dark red flowers. The yellow *I. forrestii* is a smaller form; and *I. wilsonii* is also yellow-flowered, but taller – up to 30in (75cm) in height.

IRIS CHRYSOGRAPHES

IRIS FORRESTII

44

IRISES FOR ROCK GARDENS

THERE ARE PLENTY OF EXCELLENT IRIS SPECIES, hybrids, and cultivars for the rock garden, including many of the smaller forms of those discussed in the preceding section. Many irises come from mountainous regions with poor soil, and, as a result, they adapt extremely well to broadly similar conditions in the rock garden.

Iris histrioides
This dwarf bulbous iris of the RETICULATA GROUP has large flowers that vary from light to deep violet-blue. The falls have central yellow ridges. A naturally raised position is the best place to plant some of the tinier irises, as otherwise much of the charm of the flowers would go unremarked.

45

IRIS RETICULATA 'HARMONY'

Reticulata irises

These dwarf bulbous irises need similar conditions to the Junos (see page 34) to thrive – namely plenty of sunshine, a well-drained soil, moisture in the growing season, and dry summers to give the bulbs a chance to ripen. Because they have solitary flowers, often before the leaves are fully grown, they look much better when grouped. They will not withstand very cold winters, and in harsher climates will be safer grown in pots.

There are about 10 species in the group, natives to western Asia, of which the best is *Iris reticulata* itself. In early spring, it produces solitary scented flowers that are deep purplish blue in color. It is a native to the Caucasus, but has been widely grown in many areas of the world. There are many cultivars, including 'J.S. Dijt', with reddish-purple flowers; 'Edward', which has dark-blue scented flowers with an orange ridge on the falls; 'Natascha', which has white flowers with a bluish tint; and 'George' (a hybrid between *I. reticulata* and *I. histrioides*), which has large deep-red flowers.

IRIS RETICULATA 'NATASCHA'

Earlier flowering still is *Iris histrioides* (see page 45), with large flowers that vary from light to deep violet-blue on 10cm (4in) stems. The falls have central yellow ridges.

Iris bakerana is a similar height and flowers in early spring, bearing solitary pale-blue flowers with darker-blue blotches. The leaves are narrow and almost cylindrical.

In early spring, *Iris danfordiae* bears solitary green-spotted yellow flowers on 4in (10cm) flowering stems. The bulb of this species needs to be planted deeper than other reticulatas, otherwise it may fail to flower.

IRIS RETICULATA 'GEORGE'

46

IRIS GRAMINEA

Spuria irises

The dwarf forms of the Spuria irises (discussed on page 35) flower from early to mid summer. They need a well-drained spot in the rock garden, with good soil and either full sun or light shade.

Iris graminea has attractive plum-scented purple flowers. It makes clumps of grassy leaves, and grows to about 6-8in (15-20cm) tall. *Iris kerneriana,* which grows to about 16in (40cm) in height, has up to four yellow flowers in midsummer. *Iris sintenisii* has violet-veined white flowers on stems up to l2in (30cm) tall.

IRIS SINTENISII

IRIS KERNERIANA

47

'EL TIGRE' CAL-SIB HYBRID

Pacific coast irises

The irises in the Californicae group, which interbreed readily, are made up of 11 species and innumerable hybrids between them. They need a lime-free soil and, if they are moved (which ideally they should not be), the rhizomes must be kept damp. They can be planted in early autumn about 1-2in (2-5cm) deep, and will cope with light shade.

In addition to the hybrids arising between the species in the Californicae group of irises, there are hybrids of these and the Chrysographes group (see page 44), known as Cal-sib hybrids. 'Margot Holmes', with deep reddish-purple flowers; 'El Tigre', with bronze flowers; and 'Golden Waves', with yellow flowers, are all popular garden plants. Most of the irises in the Californicae group are fairly small plants, with one or two flowers with falls that are held more horizontally than those of most irises. In mild climates, they tend to be evergreen. They usually flower from mid spring to early summer. Cultivars with names that include 'Banner' or 'Broadleigh', are particularly good.

Iris douglasiana *(below), is less demanding about conditions than most of this group of irises, and will cope with heavy or light soils and either acid or alkaline conditions. It normally bears two to three flowers, in a wide range of colors, on slender branching stems. The species ranges in height from small (6in/15cm) to tall (30in/75cm). The slender evergreen leaves are tinged with purple at their bases.*

IRIS DOUGLASIANA

48

Iris innominata is smaller, with flower stems up to 10in (25cm) tall, bearing one or two heavily veined flowers in early summer. The range of colors includes yellow, orange, white, and purple.

Iris tenax is deciduous, and is roughly the same height as *I. innominata*. It has one or two flowers, in purple, white, cream or yellow, in summer.

IRIS INNOMINATA

IRIS TENAX 'VALLEY BANNER'

IRIS RUTHENICA

IRIS UNGUICULARIS

IRIS VERNA

ROCK-GARDEN IRISES

Iris ruthenica is a tiny fragrant iris, which flowers from late spring to early summer. It has white falls that are edged with violet and violet-veined, and lavender-blue standards. This iris will tolerate light shade, and makes an excellent rock-garden plant, provided the soil does not dry out too much and is not waterlogged in winter.

The winter-flowering *Iris unguicularis* is justifiably popular, mainly on account of its attractive primrose-scented lavender flowers that bloom over a long season. It does best in full sun, in well-drained alkaline soil, but resents being moved. When grown in clumps, this iris benefits from having dead or damaged leaves removed in spring. It grows to about 10in (25cm). There are several good forms including 'Alba', with pure-white flowers.

Iris foetidissima (see page 26) is one of the easiest irises to grow, and it will tolerate light shade. Its common name is "stinking Gladwyn," owing to the smell given off by the leaves when they are crushed. Although the flowers of the species are not particularly attractive, there is a better form called 'Citrina'. It grows to about 12-24in (30-60cm). Its yellow flowers have fine brown veining, but its chief assets are the sheaves of evergreen leaves and the enormous seed pods that burst open, revealing bright-orange seeds in autumn.

The tiny *Iris verna*, only 2in (6cm) tall when in flower, has pretty lilac-blue flowers, with an orange stripe on the falls, and fans of deep-green leaves that grow taller than the flowering stems. It flowers from mid to late spring, and does well on peaty soil. It will also tolerate light shade.

Small bearded irises

There are several smaller species of bearded iris which are good candidates as front-of-border or rock-garden plants. Like the larger bearded irises (see pages 29-31), they much prefer alkaline soil and summer sun.

Iris pumila, the parent of the popular dwarf bearded cultivars, is found in Eastern Europe and Russia. The height when in flower is up to 6in (15cm), with most of that consisting of scented yellow, purple or blue flowers.

Of the miniature and standard dwarf bearded irises derived from this species, the following are particularly attractive: 'Green Spot', with creamy-white flowers and olive-green markings; 'Marhaba', with deep-blue flowers; 'Crocus', which has yellow flowers; and 'Cherry Spot', with reddish flowers.

Iris attica is an attractive small iris from the Mediterranean regions. As it is not reliably hardy, it pays to grow it in containers in colder climates. It is similar to *I. pumila* but smaller, and has small flowers in a varied range of yellows and purples.

Iris lutescens (syn *I. chamaeiris*) is another good small iris. It has large yellow or violet flowers (or a combination of both colors), and sometimes white ones. Again, it comes from the Mediterranean and flowers in early to mid spring.

Iris reichenbachii, from the mountainous regions of southern Europe, grows to about 12in (30cm) tall, and has smallish yellow or violet flowers and a yellow beard.

Iris pumila

Iris attica

Iris reichenbachii

51

IRIS CRISTATA

Small crested irises

Among the crested or Evansia group of irises (see page 38), there are two small species which make particularly good rock-garden specimens. They both grow to about 6in (15cm) tall.

Iris cristata, a native of North America, will form good-sized groups when growing well. The flowers come in various shades of lilac and blue, with a white patch in the center of the falls. As with all this group, the standards are much narrower than the falls. There are several white forms, collectively known as 'Alba'.

I. gracilipes, from Japan, grows naturally in woodland and does well on peat banks or in soil that does not dry out in summer or become waterlogged in winter. The flowers are lilac-blue with a purple-veined white center to each fall, and a white crest. There is also a white form, 'Alba'.

IRIS GRACILIPES

IRIS. GRACILIPES 'ALBA'

52

CHAPTER

III

CARE AND CULTIVATION

OH, ADAM WAS A GARDENER,
AND GOD WHO MADE HIM SEES
THAT HALF A PROPER GARDENER'S WORK
IS DONE UPON HIS KNEES.

FROM "THE GLORY OF THE GARDEN"
RUDYARD KIPLING 1865-1936

GROWING IRISES

THE IRISES MENTIONED IN CHAPTER II are all relatively easy to grow, provided they are given the right conditions (see page 58-9). These do vary from group to group, depending on whether their natural habitats are marshy swamps or dry mountainous regions of the world.

Many irises grow vigorously, eventually forming large clumps that tend to die out in the center if they are not divided and replanted fairly regularly.

Given the right environment, most irises will remain free from pests and diseases, but they are susceptible to rot if subjected to very moist conditions at the wrong time

of year. It pays to check carefully what situation and conditions will suit the particular irises you wish to grow.

Many irises make excellent cut flowers, especially if they are picked while in bud, so you can enjoy watching the flowers unfurl indoors. Among the best irises for this purpose are the English, Spanish, and Dutch irises, and the reticulatas.

General points on cultivation and propagation are discussed on the following pages, but where a group of irises or an individual species requires special attention, this is dealt with on the relevant pages in Chapter II.

Irises for borders
A magnificent colorful mixed border displaying the varieties of bearded iris, 'Lady Ilse', 'Oriental Glory', 'Redbourne', 'Ruby Wine', and 'Braithwaite'. A nicely planned well-planted iris border will provide cut flowers for indoor decoration.

PLANTING AND PROPAGATION

IRISES CAN BE INCREASED either by dividing the rhizomes or the bulbs, when the clumps are sufficiently large, or by growing new plants from seed.

Division

The advantages of division as a means of propagation are that the new plants will be identical to the parents, and new flowering-sized plants will be produced quickly. However, some plants are slow to form suitable-sized clumps, and any virus or disease that the parent plant is harboring will be transferred to the offspring.

The process of division itself couldn't be simpler – you just pull the clumps apart – but timing is important. On the whole, it is best to divide and replant after flowering, when the new roots are just starting to be made. In the case of rhizomatous irises, you can simply scrape a little of the soil away from around the rhizome to check that the new growth has started before dividing the clump.

Planting & propagating bearded irises

Remove a single rhizome from the outer edge of a clump, and cut back the leaves. Plant with the top of the rhizome level with the surface in well-drained, well-dug soil to which rotted manure has been added. Avoid putting fertilizer on top of the soil. Plant about 12in (30cm) apart.

56

Planting & propagating bulbous irises

Bulbous irises should be planted in early autumn with not less than about 4in (10cm) of soil covering the bulb. They all prefer sunny well-drained situations that dry out in mid to late summer, so that the dormant bulbs ripen well. A slow-release fertilizer is beneficial, and should be applied before planting or in the autumn in the case of established clumps. Propagation of bulbous irises is best achieved by division of clumps in early autumn.

Collecting & sowing seed

To ensure that any plants you wish to increase set seed, it helps to cross-pollinate the plants yourself. Take care to use two of the same species, to avoid creating a hybrid inadvertently. With a pair of tweezers, remove an anther from the flower selected as the male or pollen parent, and gently scrape the pollen onto the stigma of the plant selected as the female. If you then remove the outer petals from the female plant, you will ensure that a bee does not perform the same task and create a hybrid. Provided the conditions are right, the pollen will run down into the ovary and fertilize the ovules, which will develop into seeds approximately four to six weeks later. The seed is ripe and ready for sowing when the seed pod begins to split open.

The seed should be sown in a mixture of sand, peat moss, and soil, with a shallow covering of fine grit. Germination is often slow, but the seed can be sown as soon as it is ripe, and then left in the seed tray to germinate, which it will probably do in the autumn. Once seedlings are about 4in (10cm) high, they can be transplanted to more permanent positions.

Situation & Climate

IN THE WILD, IRISES GROW IN WIDELY DIFFERING CLIMATES, but for cultivation purposes you can think in terms of three simple locations – borders, water and bog, and rock gardens. Not all irises are hardy. If you want to grow some of the more tender species, you can either grow them in pots indoors (see page 60) or in an alpine house if you live in a temperate region.

Irises for borders

The plants grouped together under this heading in Chapter II are mainly the bearded irises, which cope well with dryish soil. The Spuria irises and some of the other border irises, such as the Evansia group, need more moisture than the bearded ones. If planted in a mixed herbaceous border, all these irises will grow well if they are not too closely packed together, allowing air and sunlight to filter through in the summer. This will help the rhizomes to ripen and set flowers the following year. On the whole these irises cannot cope with badly drained soil, so any soils that are heavy or impermeable should have grit and humus worked into them.

An engraving of an iris border from a 19th-century gardening manual.

Irises for water & bog gardens

Those irises that originate in the wild in marshy conditions make excellent subjects for the water or bog garden, but some of them are quite fussy as to the amount of water they require. The true water-loving species, which thrive in about 2in (5cm) of water, include many of the Japanese irises, *I. pseudacorus, I. virginica,* and *I. versicolor* (the latter will also cope well in moist soil only).

All these irises prefer rich soil, and it helps to add plenty of well-rotted manure when they are planted.

Irises for rock gardens

Many of the smaller irises, including most of those which grow naturally in the mountains, as well as some of the hybrids, will do well in rock gardens, where good drainage helps to prevent the rhizomes or bulbs from rotting away. Most prefer a near-neutral soil with plenty of grit and not too much humus. Those requiring warm sun are the reticulatas, the small Junos, and the dwarf bearded irises. The small crested irises prefer cooler, damper conditions, but they still need good drainage. Some of the smaller Pacific coast irises also do well in the rock garden, but do not like highly alkaline conditions.

59

Container-grown irises

Many of the smaller irises can be grown as indoor plants. The small bulbous irises – the reticulatas – are the best subjects for this purpose, but most of the dwarf bearded irises will perform equally well.

Planting in containers

The bulbs should be planted in a large container outside in mid autumn. Use a well-drained soilless compost to which some fine grit has been added. Once the bulbs start to show signs of growth, transplant them into smaller pots suitable for indoor use, and then bring them indoors to flower.

After flowering, the bulbs can be replanted outside again, and will flower the following year, provided they are fed regularly while the leaves are dying down.

To reduce the risk of ink-spot disease, which is always a danger with reticulata irises, make sure the containers are thoroughly cleaned before they are reused.

Cut flowers

Dutch, English, and Spanish irises make particularly good subjects for spring and early-summer flower arrangements. Dutch irises normally flower in late spring, but they can be forced to provide flowers after Christmas. Spanish irises flower a few weeks after the Dutch, and English irises bloom in midsummer.

When cutting irises for flower arrangements, try to leave as much foliage on the plant as possible, and cut them just as the first flower bud is about to unfurl. The remaining buds will then open indoors. On the whole, irises look best arranged on their own, as many famous paintings bear witness. Provided they are given a regular supply of fresh water, they will last for at least a week.

Container-grown irises
Although the little Iris danfordiae, with its attractive yellow flowers, can be grown in open ground, it does not like extreme winters and is best grown indoors if you live in a harsh climate.

Indoor floral display
Garden-grown irises can be cut to provide a fairly long-lasting indoor display provided a few simple rules are observed (see opposite). The display below shows a delightful arrangement of commercially grown Dutch irises.

61

Diseases & pests

IRISES ARE NOT PARTICULARLY SUSCEPTIBLE to disease or predators, although aphids and slugs can be destructive. Some of the common problems and their remedies are described below.

Rhizome rot

The most common problem affecting irises is rhizome rot. Rhizome rot is often caused by overwatering or poorly drained soil, or by very wet summers. Eventually, if left untreated, it will kill the entire clump. The first signs are normally the leaves turning yellow and the flower stalks starting to wilt. If you check, you will probably discover that the rhizomes are beginning to go soft and mushy. Treatment is relatively simple. Cut away affected leaves and rhizome until only healthy tissue remains. Dust the cut surfaces with dry Bordeaux mixture, then burn all infected material and sterilize the knife.

Leaf spot

Small black spots start to appear on the leaves, particularly of bearded irises, and eventually the leaves will wither if untreated. This will not kill the plants, but it is disfiguring. To prevent it occurring, remove any dead leaves on and around the iris bed in autumn. Where it does occur, spray the plants with a copper fungicide or a systemic fungicide such as benomyl.

Gray mold

Beardless irises are sometimes susceptible to gray mold, which turns the leaf tips brown. Gray mold can also be detected at the bases of the leaves. Spray the affected plants with benomyl or a similar fungicide.

Ink-spot disease

This affects the bulbous irises, and the first visible symptom is that the leaves turn yellow prematurely. If you dig up the bulb, it will have black spots or streaks. There is no cure, but it can be prevented by dipping bulbs in benomyl before planting them.

Slugs & aphids

These can be as much of a problem for irises as other plants, and should be treated in the usual way. Aphid attacks can sometimes result in the plants being infected with a virus, particularly iris mosaic virus, for which there is no cure. So look out for aphids and eradicate them promptly.

Societies & Shows

THROUGHOUT THE WORLD there are societies dedicated to spreading knowledge and interest in irises. Most of them date back at least to the period after the First World War, or possibly earlier.

National & international societies

The American Iris Society, founded in 1930, publishes a quarterly bulletin with up-to-date information, and it also registers the names of all new irises, as well as publishing a list of these registrations. In addition, it holds garden trials, and gives awards for all classes of iris.

One of the best-known international iris shows is organized by the Italian Iris Society (the Società Italiana dell'Iris) in collaboration with the city of Florence. Of the awards given internationally, the Primo Firenze (or Gold Florin) is the most coveted in the iris world.

Showing irises

If you are considering submitting irises for an award, the following criteria are essential. According to Cassidy and Linnegar in *Growing Irises*, your plants should have: straight stems; well-spaced branches; three or more flowers open; a clean break where the first flower has been removed; clean (not spotty) foliage; clean, unbruised flowers; and a well-supported stem.

Such is the single-mindedness of the dedicated iris fancier that even art does not match up to nature, as Harry Randall wrote in *Irises*, admittedly with tongue in cheek: "Although I greatly admire the work of van Gogh, I cannot enthuse over his iris paintings. The one dated 1889 has the stem awkwardly falling over, the dead flowers have not been removed – a terrible omission for a tidy gardener – and the colours are drab compared with those seen at the Chelsea Flower Show."

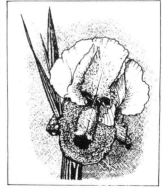

BIBLIOGRAPHY

Many books and journals have been consulted,
and the following will be found to make useful and pleasurable reading:

Flower Chronicles Hollingsworth, Rutgers Press U.S.A. 1958
Iris for Every Garden Sydney B. Mitchell, Barrows 1949
Iris Harry Randell, Batsford 1969
The Iris Brian Mathew, Batsford 1981
The Genus Iris W.R. Dykes, Cambridge University Press 1913
The Iris John C. Wister, *Farm and Garden Library*,
Orange Judd Publishing Company 1930
Growing Irises Cassidy and Linnegar, Croom Helm 1982
Irises F.F. Rockwell, Macmillan 1928
The Iris Book Molly Price, Van Nostrand 1965

ACKNOWLEDGMENTS

The producers gratefully acknowledge the following individuals,
organizations, and sources that have assisted in the
creation of this book.

FOR THE SUPPLY OF PHOTOGRAPHS :
Brian Mathew.
The International Bloembollen Center,
Hillegom, The Netherlands.
Pat Brindley, Horticultural Picture Library,
Cheltenham, Gloucestershire, U.K.
FOR THE CREATION OF ORIGINAL ILLUSTRATIONS:
Julia Cobbold
FOR THE COLORING & ENHANCEMENT OF ARCHIVE ILLUSTRATIONS:
Robin Harris & David Day
FOR PICTORIAL REFERENCES AND VISUAL MATERIAL:
The Natural History of Plants Kerner & Oliver,
The Gresham Publishing Co. 1904
The Gardener's Assistant William Watson,
The Gresham Publishing Co. 1908
The Dover Pictorial Archive series
Botanical Prints Norman & Eve Robinson,
Studio Editions 1990
The Gardeners' and Poultry Keepers' Guide & Catalogue
William Cooper 1900
William Morris Wallpapers Peggy Vance,
Bracken Books 1989
The Art of Heraldry Arthur Charles Fox-Davies 1904
Reprinted by Bracken Books as *Heraldic Designs* 1989
English Flower Garden & Home Grounds W. Robinson,
John Murray 1883
Shirley Curzon
William Morris, Iris Design Cup & Saucer on page 14
reproduced by kind permission.
Cup and saucer produced under licence by
Nikko Company for the Victoria & Albert Museum
William Morris Collection 1991